Courage to Succeed

Succeed

A Big Girl Now

Gwendolyn H. Moore

ISBN: 978-0-9888644-4-3
Library of Congress Control Number: 2014951076

Edited by: Dolly Ogawa-Amst
Cover Design: Juan Roberts, Creative Lunacy
Interior Design: John Sibley,
Rock Solid Productions

Published by:
Knowledge Power Books
Valencia, California 91355
www.knowledgepowerbooks.com

Printed in the United States of America

I'm dedicating this book to Rita who showed such unquestionable fortitude and determination as she strove to complete her educational goals.

I would like to thank my husband and sons for their encouragement and patience with me as I attempted to write this piece.

Table of Contents

Chapter One

READY OR NOT

(*Pages from a journal.*)

I am a fourteen-year old Hispanic girl whose parents married me off to this man who was about seven years older than me. Marriage was not quite what I thought it would be, and it's not what I wanted to do at the time. I wanted to hang out with my girls at the mall, talk about the boys in my class, and go to dances. I wanted to go to school. In fact, I was pretty good in school, but Momma said that Alonzo would take good care of me and he was a good man. So I married him.

I'm still in school, but my stomach and back hurts and my chest looks like two cassava melons. What is wrong with me? Uh, I feel like I'm going to throw up! I can't remember if I had a period or not this month. Could I be pregnant? No, I can't be pregnant! I don't know what to do first. Should I tell someone? Aw man, I don't know anything about having a baby. Maybe I'm not pregnant. I'll talk to my girl, Gaby. She'll know what to do.

I met Gaby after school and as we walked home, I began to tell her what was going on with me. When I told her that I thought that I might be pregnant, she swallowed her gum and bucked her eyes. Then she said, "Girl, have you told your mom or Alonzo?

"No," I said. "Alonzo doesn't really want any babies right now." Gaby asked me if I was sure. I said no.

Then Gaby said, "I know this place Anita told me about that will check you out. Let's go over there after school tomorrow. It's a walk-in-clinic."

"Ok," I said.

"Angelica Ortiz?" That's me. No one ever calls me by my whole name except my teachers. I've got to remember I'm not in school now. I ease out of my seat. Gaby looks at me as I stand up. I'm so scared. I feel like somebody's holding my nose and I can't breathe. I blow and breathe real hard as I stand to follow the nurse. I guess that's what she is.

The doctor is a tall guy with red hair. I don't know this man. I never seen him or this woman before in my life and they're telling me to take off my clothes and put this big shirt, oh yeah, gown on. The doctor had me put my feet up in this whatever, and then he looked down "there." Then he put his hands down there, too and looked and felt my stomach.

I was so embarrassed. Then this woman gave me a paper cup and told me to pee in it. For what? Now I wonder what Gaby would do about now. I went to the bathroom. Dang! I just peed all over my hand! Peeing in this little cup isn't as easy as it looks.

This woman, the nurse came back into the room and told me to get dressed and wait for the doctor. So I put my things on and sat quietly on

3

this cot and swung my legs back and forth as I waited for the doctor.

The doctor came in with a folder and looked at me. He told me his name and started asking me a lot of questions. "How old are you?" he asked. I know he knows how old I am. He just wants me to say it.

So I said, "fourteen."

Then the doctor said, "I see you have a ring on, are you married?"

"Yes," I said, I got married three months ago."

Then the doctor said, "And your parents know about this?"

"My mom and dad told me it was okay. They made me." I said. The doctor sat down and shook his head and then opened the folder.

"Well, it looks like you're two months pregnant. How do you feel?" He asked.

"All right I guess. My head, stomach and chi-chis hurt." "Did you tell your mother how you felt?" "No."

The doctor said, "Well, you should tell her. Here's a prescription for some prenatal vitamins. You need to take one every day and then come see me once a month if you want to have a healthy baby."

I took the prescription from him and the nurse made me stop at the front desk to make my next appointment. So I made one for the next month on a Wednesday after school because I didn't want to miss any classes.

Gaby was still waiting for me in the waiting room. She jumped up when I came out and started asking me all sorts of questions. "Well, what did the doctor say? Are you pregnant? How many months? Is it a boy or girl? When are you going to have it?"

I told her, "Yes, I am pregnant. But girl, you can't believe they gave me a little cup to pee in. You know I put as much pee on the floor as I did in the cup." We both laughed about that. "He said that I was two months. I guess I better tell Alonzo and Momma. She can tell Papa." I said.

Sharing the News

Alonzo was still at work when I got home. So I went over to my mom's house. Momma looked at me and then asked, "How many months are you?" I still don't know how she knew because I wasn't even showing. She asked me if I had told Alonzo yet.

"No," I said, "but I am going to."

Then Momma started telling me how my chest and stomach were going to get bigger and that my hips were going to get wider because the women in our family carry their babies in their hips, too. Now that sounded dumb to me because I always thought that women carried babies in their stomachs. Oh well, I told Momma everything the doctor said. Momma just smiled. Alonzo really didn't want a baby right then, but I guess the more he thought about it, the more he liked the idea about being a daddy. I started to show a little.

Some Changes

Gaby was a good friend. She never told anyone what happened at the clinic that day. The kids at school started pointing at me and began whispering about me.

I didn't tell them that I was married, but I guess someone did, because one day Maria asked me how it felt to be married and pregnant at fourteen. "Who told you?" It was hard to tell that I was pregnant because I wasn't real big. I used to wear a size three.

The teachers started asking me what I was going to do about school and the baby. I really wasn't sure. All I knew was that I wanted to go to school as long as I could. I finally told the office that I was married. Naturally they didn't believe me. They even had someone call my mom. They had to get a translator because Momma didn't speak English. She told the school that I was married and had been married for about six months, but I never changed my name on anything at school. Now I had to change my last

7

name if I wanted to keep going to school. Alonzo didn't see what the problem was. He didn't finish school and he couldn't figure out why school was so important to me.

Chapter Two

LABOR

Boy! I'm getting huge. I don't know how I'm going to get to English before the bell rings. I can't run and this baby is hurting my back. Whew! I made it. Miss Thatcher lets me sit at the desk by the door.

I've got to turn in my homework before I forget. I almost didn't finish it. I was so tired and sleepy last night. Alonzo is at work now. I'll get home before he comes home. I'll try to cook before I do my schoolwork.

Maybe he won't get mad if he sees food on the table when he gets home. I'll finish my schoolwork when he goes out. He never tells me where he's going. So I stopped asking him. I don't care! Let him go out!

What? What is this? I'm wet! There's water coming out of me. Something's wrong. I'll call Momma. She'll know what's happening.

She came right over. I sat down and grabbed my stomach. "Oh, that hurts. Momma, I'm hurting down there. Oh no here comes another pain." Momma, what's happening to me? What should I do? Ouch, it hurts. Oh this really hurts."

Momma asked me how long had I been hurting. I tried to tell her about the water coming out and the pains that came afterwards, but I kept having pains. It felt like someone was kicking my butt with metal tipped boots on. "Oh, there's another one."

Momma figured that the pains were coming about every ten minutes. So she grabbed my coat and put it on me and drove me to the hospital.

They asked me a lot of questions, at the hospital, that I couldn't answer, because I couldn't think of anything but all the pain that was kicking my butt. Momma called Papa and he and Alonzo came together. Alonzo came running down the hall looking for me.

The nurse asked who my doctor was. I was hurting so bad that I couldn't remember his name at first. Then I said, "Dr. Campman." So I guess they called him. They took me to a room, put a gown on me, and laid me on this bed that had poles at the foot. Oh that really hurts. "Momma, Momma."

I'm screaming and crying now because I have never felt pain like this before. Cramps are nothing compared to this. It feels like a truck has hit me and is dragging me along.

Alonzo is standing against the wall looking like he wants to cry. For what? He isn't feeling all this pain! I looked at him and started to get mad. "You did this to me," I screamed.

Dr. Campman came into the room and asked how I was doing. He looked at my chart. Then he started feeling my stomach and began looking at my "junk."

Oh man, here comes another one. "Ouch, ouch, ouch!" Okay, I don't care what you're looking at. Just get this baby out of me. "Momma, Momma, it hurts. It hurts so bad," I said. Then a nurse came in and put my feet in these hoops. The doctor felt my stomach again and looked up in my "stuff" again.

The nurse told me to push. The doctor said, "That's right. Now push again. I can see the head. He's crowning."

I didn't know what he meant, but I started pushing as hard as I could. The more I pushed the more I wanted to push.

Alonzo's face was wet. Is he crying? Momma wiped my face.

Finally, I heard a baby crying. It's my baby! It's a boy! He's kind of cute. Why is he so wrinkled looking, and what's that crap all over him? He weights 6 lbs. and 2 oz. That's kind of big I think. Alonzo wants to name the baby after him. I don't care. I'm just glad it's over. I only stayed in the hospital for two days. They asked me before I left if I was going to breast feed the baby. I said, "Breast what?" "No way!" Just thinking about it made me want to hurl!

Momma said that I needed to stay home for a little while, but I wanted to go back to school. I didn't want to get that far behind. Gaby brought me my homework every day. I think she really wanted to see the baby.

Alonzo must be crazy if he thinks we're going to do it tonight! That's how Little Alonzo got here. So I said, "No, "H…" no! He was mad, but he'll get over it. He stamped out the house. I don't even care.

My baby is just a week old and my butt still hurts. I look around our apartment and wonder how can I do all this work and take care of the baby too, because I am going back to school. I don't care if the apartment is dirty and dinner is not cooked.

Back to School

Alonzo's pretty much accepted the fact that I'm going back to school. He still can't understand why, though.

Momma keeps the baby. I grab him on the way back from school. I feed him. Then I fix some food for Alonzo and me. This sucks, but I got to do it. I started letting Alonzo touch me. But he better be careful 'cause I don't want another baby. School is great and Little Alonzo is getting so big and fat. He's so cute and he's mine. Alonzo goes out almost every night after he eats. I asked him where he was going one time and he got mad at me and started yelling about how he didn't have to tell me nothing cause it wasn't my business. So I stopped asking him after that.

Oh, I've just about caught up on all of my subjects at school. I don't know how I did it. Dang! That baby's crying again. Why won't he shut up! I already fed him. What does he want? I can't just sit and hold him. Okay, okay boy! I've got you. Now shut up! Three more weeks before school is out, and then I will have more time for this baby and Alonzo.

Eleventh Grade!

Well, I got through a whole year and a summer and school is starting again. I'm in the eleventh grade. Little Alonzo is fifteen months old. He's walking and trying to talk and everything. Alonzo picks him up and just grins when he says, "Da Da." Everybody says the baby looks just like his daddy. That just makes Alonzo grin from ear to ear. I, personally, think Little Alonzo is cuter. He has my nose and eyes though, I can't forget how much pain that baby gave me. So Alonzo can just stop strutting around like he did something special. I was the one who did all of the work.

Keeping Up

Momma keeps Little Alonzo while I'm at school. So I drop him off every morning after

Alonzo goes to work. Thank God we live in the flat right above her and Papa. I usually walk to school if the weather is good.

My classes are not bad. Algebra sucks though. I have six classes in all. I try to get home in time to cook and have food ready for Alonzo when he comes home. I try to feed the baby while we eat. We play with the baby a little while and then I bathe him and put him to bed. Alonzo's going out again tonight. I almost asked him where he was going, but I changed my mind.

I start on my homework and Alonzo gets home around 2:00 a.m., and was rubbing on me. He wanted to have sex. He seems to want to do it after he comes home every night. He thinks he's got it going on, but he ain't all that. He's all right. Man I'm too tired. I have school tomorrow. Momma says having sex is my "wifely duty." Not when it's 2:00 a.m. in the morning though! I'll try. I don't want to fight with Alonzo. I have to get up at 6:00 a.m. I'll drag my tired butt out of bed and get ready for school in the morning.

Chapter Three

TWO YEARS LATER

We gave Little Alonzo a birthday party. He turned two years old today. He's laughing and running from one person to the other. Alonzo brought out the birthday cake, but before he could put the cake on the table, Little Alonzo had stuck his fingers in the icing and was licking the icing off as he spread it all over his face. I had to take a picture of him. He looked so funny! Papa laughed at him as he picked him up to look at his little dirty face.

I started to cut a piece of cake. Then I got so dizzy that I had to grab a chair and sit down. Momma looked at me funny. I started crying. Alonzo came in and looked at me like I was crazy. I'm sixteen. I can't have two kids and still go to school. I can't go through this whole thing again, but I feel the same way I did with Little Alonzo. Aw man! No way!

I woke up Saturday with puffy eyes and Little Alonzo was asking for some milk. Alonzo didn't know what to do or say to me. He just walked around staring at me like I was weird or something. I knew I had maybe missed a month or two, but I thought I had miss-counted or something. So, to make sure, I made an appointment with Dr. Campman for Thursday after school.

I left school in a hurry Thursday. Gaby didn't go with me this time. I had to go through the same old crazy stuff again – the open gown, peeing in the cup, and putting my legs up in those metal hoops at the end of the cot. I still feel embarrassed when Dr. Campman starts feeling my stomach and looking up my, "you know what." I can't even look him in the eye when he asks me questions. The nurse stayed in the room this time and told me to get dressed after the doctor finished. I grabbed my stuff and dressed as fast as I could.

Dr. Campman came back into the room and just looked at me. He still didn't want to believe that I was married until I showed the nurse my insurance card that I got from Alonzo.

The doctor told me that I was eight weeks pregnant. I dragged myself out of the office and walked slowly down the street toward the bus stop. A couple of kids I knew from school passed me. I think they said hi. I'm not sure.

Not Again

I couldn't think about anything else but what that doctor said, "You're two months pregnant." Just thinking about it made me cry. I finally reached Momma's house. Papa was still at work. Good. I didn't want him to hear what I had to tell Momma.

Momma looked at me and started crying, too. "Well, how long are you?" Momma asked.

Between sobs I finally said, "Two months."
Momma just sat and stared at me crying. I don't
know if she was thinking about how it was back in
the day when she was my age and having kids or
not. She got married young, too. "Momma, what
am I going to do?" I asked.

"You're going to have this baby. We're
Catholic. You can't kill it!" she said. I sat down
and started crying again. Momma said, "Girl stop
that crying now and wipe your face. You have a
man who works and takes care of you."

"But Momma," I said, "sometimes he won't
touch me until he wants to have sex. He doesn't
talk to me or nothing and when I ask him where
he's been or where he's going, he just gets mad
and starts yelling at me."

Then Momma said something I couldn't
understand. She said, "Girl you don't ask Alonzo
where he's going or where he's been. Your job is
to please him and give him whatever he wants
and not ask questions." I said, "But he won't even
take care of the baby when he's home. He won't

even pick up a piece of paper off the floor." "Because that's your job," Momma said. "And you think I want to have another baby to strap me down?" I said. "He wants sex all the time, the house clean and food cooked, and he won't lift a finger to help me around this place, and don't mention school to him. It's not my fault he quit school after the tenth grade. He really wants me to quit school, too. But I'm not quitting school. I am going to graduate! I don't care what it takes!"

Chapter Four

THE NEW ADDITION

Katina was born just after I turned seventeen. She's cute and weighed 6 lbs. 8 oz. She has a head full of black hair and dimples. No doubt Little Alonzo thinks she's a toy. I've got to really watch him cause I caught him trying to pick her up. Momma comes over every day. She's really a big help.

I stayed home for a couple of weeks, and then I went back to school. Momma kept both babies for me. I don't know what I would have done without her. School will be out in about ten weeks. I can't wait.

Maybe I can get a job this summer. Who am I kidding? I barely have time to brush my teeth. It looks like I'm going to pass to the twelfth grade though, and my grades are not too shabby either. Alonzo really likes Katina, but he won't change her diaper or anything. I'm trying to potty train Little Alonzo between housework and schoolwork. Two kids in diapers is no joke, and don't think about how much those pampers cost. I haven't got any new stuff in about a year.

Alonzo is still going out after he eats. I just look at him. I don't ask any questions. He came back at 12:00 a.m. tonight. The babies and I were sleep, but he woke me up feeling all over me tying to get me to have sex with him. I think he is drunk, too. His breath stinks. Dang!

I can't believe I'm now in the twelfth grade! Now, if I can just stay in school and not get pregnant. My classes are harder, but I've got to pass them. I've made it this far. I like running. So I tried out for the track team and made it. I don't know how I'm going to make the meets. I'll worry about that when they come up.

I learned how to make tortillas. Momma showed me when I went to pick up the kids from school. Alonzo ate three of them. I'm becoming a pretty good cook. I couldn't boil water when we first got married. Now I can make a lot of stuff. Little Alonzo's almost three. He finally goes to the bathroom by himself. Thank God!

Katina's trying to walk and talk. She can say "Da Da." I don't know why. Her daddy doesn't spend much time with her. She's funny though. She tries to take Little Alonzo's toys from him. He hits her and takes it back. Naturally she starts screaming like he broke her arm or something. Alonzo thinks this is so funny and just pats Little Alonzo's head. I picked up Katina and tried to shut her up. I rocked her, I Patted her, then I give her another toy. She stopped crying and began to play again. I am so glad because that screaming was working my nerves. She and Little Alonzo have got to learn how to play together.

Homework, Housework

I made some beef burritos and refried beans for dinner. It was pretty good. I fed the kids, then

Alonzo ate and watched TV and then he left. I folded the clothes and put them away. After that I washed the dishes and sat down with the kids. I tried to read them a story, but Katina won't sit still that long. Little Alonzo likes me to read to him, though. We played with the blocks. Then I bathed them. Yeah, I bathe them together. Katina wanted me to hold her longer, but I have homework to do. I held her for a little while longer then gave her a bottle of milk. She finally laid down and went to sleep. Now I can write this paper. "No, Alonzo, you can't have some water. Go to sleep."

No Prom for Me

Everybody's shopping for their prom dresses. I wish I could go to the prom, but I know Alonzo won't let me. So I won't even ask him if I can go. Besides, who would take me? What would I wear? Alonzo sure wouldn't buy me a dress, and escorting me to the prom is just out of the question. He says I shouldn't even talk to other boys since I'm married. He caught me saying "Hi" to this guy from one of my classes and he went nuts. He said I was seeing other guys. I tried to tell him that I wasn't, but he acted like he didn't even believe me. I told Momma what he said, and she just shook her head.

Papa told me to get off the track team, so I did. I quit the track team, but I'm not quitting school. I don't care what Alonzo says. I'm trying to keep everything together and I think I'm doing a pretty good job. I pay the bills, fix the food, take care of the children, clean the apartment and go to school.

All Alonzo does is go to work, come home and eat, and then go and stay out half the night. Something's wrong with this picture. It's not fair! I'm going to study hard and pass these exams, because I am going to graduate from high school.

Chapter Five

GRADUATION!

Today's a special day. It's graduation day! They're passing out our caps and gowns. I can't believe it! I'm marching across the stage and getting my diploma! Momma and Papa came with the kids. Alonzo said he had to work, but I see he's here too along with my brothers and sisters.

I'm so happy I could scream. Miss Hines, my counselor, said I did so well that some college wants to give me a scholarship. Can you imagine that? The music is starting to play. The counselors started to line us up. About two hundred kids are walking today. It's still hard for me to think that I'm one of the two hundred.

I'm standing in line thinking about all the

29

people I need to thank for helping me get to this day. Momma kept my kids. My teachers let me make up the work I missed. The counselors helped me choose the right classes, and Alonzo's "I don't care" attitude made me more determined to finish school.

Oops, I missed a step. I'm in the sixth row. I wonder why they always play that same lame song at every graduation? But today it sounds pretty cool to me. I'm sitting now listening to the speaker. He just made a joke and everybody's laughing. I'm so nervous and scared that I might trip or fall when they call my name until I almost can't hear what the speaker's saying. Everyone's clapping. He finally finished.

They've started calling the seniors' name in alphabetical order. I didn't know that there were so many Gonzales' in my graduating class. OMG! They've gotten to my row! We're standing. We're walking to the stage. My legs don't work! "Come on legs move! Get to steppin!" The counselor calls my name "Angelica Ortiz." I hear my sisters and brothers shouting out my name. I'm kind of embarrassed. I can't look over where they're sitting because I'm afraid I'll stumble or even worse, fall. So I keep walking towards the stage. I manage to walk up the steps without tripping. I turned and shook the counselor's hand as he handed me my diploma.

When I turned to walk off the stage, I saw Alonzo taking my picture. I waved my diploma in the air and gave a quick smile as I stepped down the stairs. When all the names were called, and they told us that we were the graduating class for that year, we screamed and threw our caps up in the air. I sure hope I can find mine. Oh, there it is, I'm going to frame this cap.

Celebration!

Maria and Gaby graduated, too. We grabbed each other as we screamed and danced around. This is just unreal! They asked me if I wanted to go with them and their family to celebrate, but before I could answer Papa came over and told me that we were all going to dinner at Red Lobster. I couldn't believe it! We have never gone out to dinner as a family! When I passed my old teachers, they all congratulated me. I grinned and thanked them as I walked out the door to the car.

"I'm so proud of you." Momma said.

Ricky, my brother asked me, "What's next?" I told him that I really want to go to college.

My sisters just looked at me and laughed. They both have husbands, kids and no high school diplomas. Their husbands tell them what to do and when to do it. I just can't live like that anymore. I'm going to get a job this summer.

Alonzo is not going to like that. He wants me home all the time. I need things and so do the kids.

Chapter Six

THE JOURNEY CONTINUES

I've started a new chapter in my life. I worked at the factory, but that work was too hard. So I got a job working for the school district. I've been going to college, too. I've got two years under my belt even though I had another baby. Yeah, I had another little "rug rat." I had another boy. I ran out of my birth control pills, and well, the rest is history. Momma keeps the kids while I go to college. I'm doing well in my classes and I was placed on the dean's list. They will pay for my classes if I keep my grades up.

Alonzo can't deal with me getting all of this education. He tried to tell me to quit. He's always trying to tell me what to do. He even almost hit me. Now, that would have been a big mistake, because he or no other man is going to hit me. He yells at me and we seem to argue all of the time. He still refuses to tell me where he's going at night. He told me it was none of my "D" business.

Then he started calling me all sorts of ugly names. He told me that I thought I was something special when all I am is "poo caca" under his shoe. We have been fussing and arguing for months now. Then I found out that he had been cheating on me for years, the dog.

Ending and Beginning

So I divorced Alonzo. Momma just couldn't understand why I divorced him. After all, Momma says, "Alonzo has a job. He comes home every night and he takes care of his family."

Ha! He wants a slave, and I refuse to be treated like a slave. I can't think for myself, I have to obey him without asking questions. Alonzo or no other man is going to talk to me or treat me any old way and wipe his feet on me like I'm a rug or doormat. I'm going to concentrate on my studies; become a teacher; and take care of my kids. I've had to grow up fast. The little girl doesn't exist anymore. I'm a woman now with real goals and responsibilities. I've come a long way and I still have a few more miles to go, but I am going to make it. I am going to SUCCEED!

About the Author

Gwendolyn H. Moore grew up in a small city in Michigan with seven brothers and one sister. Being the eldest, she was often called the "second mom" as she taught her siblings the skills she knew and loved. She had such a love for learning and reading that she pursued a career in education. After teaching for a number of years and loving literature so much, Gwendolyn decided to put some of her thoughts and experiences in writing for other young readers to enjoy. "Courage to Succeed" is just one of many she chose to share.